LOOK AND FIND

LOOK AND FIND

It's time for a road trip! But will everything fit into the Toon Car? Look around to find these on-the-go items:

Look at the items in the colored border. Can you find them in the big picture? When you're finished, check the corner for another challenge!

"Which way to these colorful things? Can you spot them all?"

orange ball — purple bow — yellow box
blue bag — pink purse — red car — 7

6

WHAT'S DIFFERENT?

WHAT'S DIFFERENT?

Sand is grand, and sun is fun!

Look for 20 differences between these seaside scenes

When you see a pair of pictures, try to find what's different. There are 10 or 20 differences between each pair. Can you spot them all?

17

16

answers on page 21

3

LOOK AND FIND

Meeska, mooska, it's Mickey Mouse and the rest of the Clubhouse crew! Who? See if you can find all of these friends:

4

"The Clubhouse garden is full of flowers! Can you find and count these bee-yooty-ful blooms?"

1 2 3 4

LOOK AND FIND

It's time for a road trip! But will everything fit into the Toon Car? Look around to find these on-the-go items:

"Which way to these colorful things?
Can you spot them all?"

orange ball   purple bow   yellow box

blue bag   pink purse   red car   7

LOOK AND FIND

The Clubhouse crew is planning another field trip. Can you guess where the pals are going? Maybe these things will give you a clue:

Pluto found 1 rocket. Can you find and count these other space souvenirs?

2 globes

3 space posters

4 books

5 crescent cookies

6 alien toys

9

LOOK AND FIND

Beep, beep! The wheels on the bus go round and round. Will you look around for these streetside somethings?

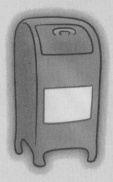

"You can count on finding these numbers around the bus stop. Do you see them all?"

1 2 3 4 5 6 7 8 9 10

WHAT'S DIFFERENT?

Here in the rainforest, it's an animal extravaganza!

WHAT'S DIFFERENT?

Hot diggity dog! Minnie loves a lunchtime picnic. Mickey does, too.

There are 10 differences in these pictures. Look closely to find each one.

Sand is grand,
and sun is fun!

Look for 20 differences between these seaside scenes.

Welcome to SANDY BEACH

WHAT'S DIFFERENT?

Goofy's camera will catch all the details.

Will you spot them, too? Find 10 differences between the pictures.

answers on page 21

WHAT'S DIFFERENT?

answers for
pages 12 - 13

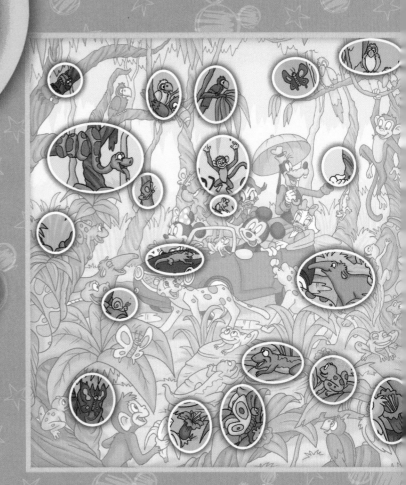

answers for
pages 14 - 15

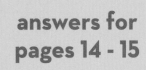

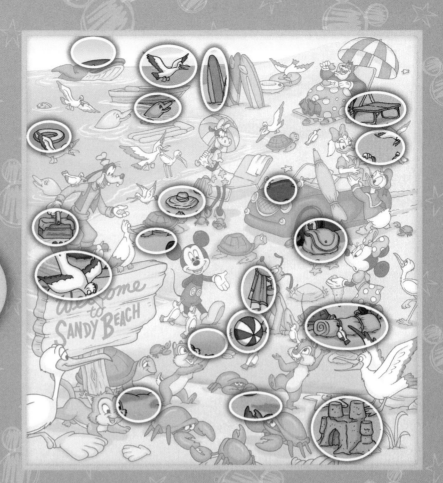

answers for pages 16 - 17

Welcome to SANDY BEACH

answers for pages 18 - 19

LOOK AND FIND

It's up, up, and away in the Glove Balloon! Keep your eyes on the skies and find these cloud shapes:

22

"My oh my! What do you spy in these places?"

under the balloon   next to the pier

above the balloon   over the coconut tree

LOOK AND FIND

Splishity-splash! Everyone's having fun on the water. Can you find these things that float?

"Get into the swim of things and find these shapes around the water."

● circle   ■ square   ◆ diamond

▲ triangle   ★ star   ⬡ hexagon

LOOK AND FIND

All aboard the Choo Choo Express! Can you track down these things at the train station?

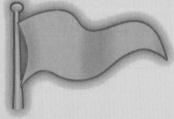

Train Schedule
1:00 PM
4:00 PM

26

Train
Schedule
1:00 PM
4:00 PM

Apple
Festival
this
weekend

"All right! Train begins with the letter T. It's time to look for these things that start with T, too."

LOOK AND FIND

There's a lot to see under the sea! Can you spot all of these underwater friends?

"A-hyuck! Let's dive down into the deep and count some colorful fish."

4 red fish   5 yellow fish   6 blue fish

WHAT'S DIFFERENT?

Inside, outside, all around: it's a busy day at the Clubhouse!

answers on page 38

Mickey Park is the perfect place for a picnic.

Look for 10 differences between these scenes.

answers on page 38

WHAT'S DIFFERENT?

The Toon Car has a flat tire—and Toodles has a Mouseketool to fix it!

Can you spot all 20 differences between these pictures?

Mickey loves to paint, and Pluto loves to help!

Can you find the 10 differences between these pictures?

answers on page 39

37

WHAT'S DIFFERENT?

answers for
pages 30 - 31

answers for
pages 32 - 33

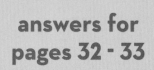

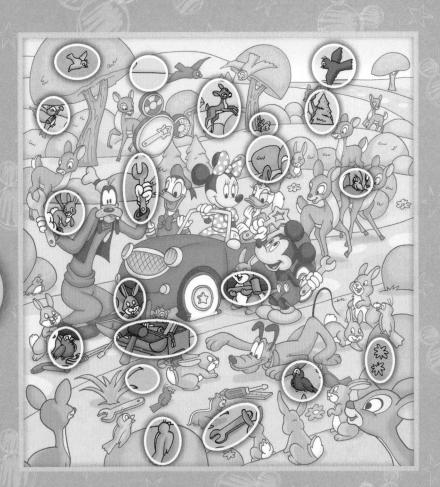

answers for
pages 34 - 35

answers for
pages 36 - 37

LOOK AND FIND

Professor von Drake can't decide which he likes better: apple pie or pumpkin? While he thinks about it, look for these things around the farm:

"It's rhyme time! Yep, rhyme time! Can you help Chip and me find things that rhyme with these words?"

sky / pie   boat / goat   cake / rake

hat / cat   bee / tree   pen / hen   41

LOOK AND FIND

Zip, zoom, zing! The gang is on the go today. Can you find these things that move?

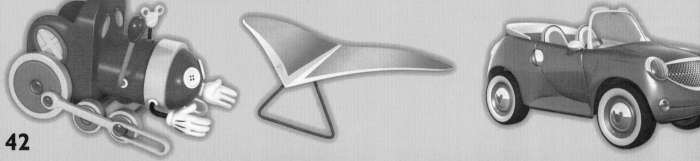

Stop and look for these shapes in the picture:

● circle ▬ rectangle

▲ triangle ◗ oval

43

LOOK AND FIND

The Mousekenauts aren't the only travelers in outer space. Can you spot these other orbiting objects?

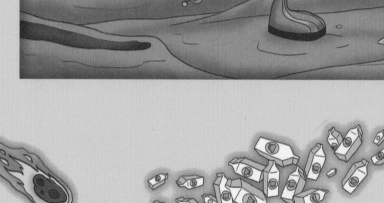

"Mousekenaut Mickey to Earth station:
do you see these things?"

LOOK AND FIND

When everyone chips in, spring cleaning at the Clubhouse is fast and fun. Look for these things that help the crew clean up:

"Spring into action and find these things that rhyme with spring!"

ring   swing   string   king

LOOK AND FIND

Willie the Giant loves his giant-sized toys! Can you spot these favorites from his toy box?

When Willie can't find baseball equipment his own size,
he uses these things instead. Can you spot them all?

a house (for home plate)   a telephone pole (for a bat)
a golf green (for first base)   a water tank (for a baseball)

Look for 20 differences between these dance-o-riffic scenes.

WHAT'S DIFFERENT?

Tomatoes or potatoes? What's Donald planting?

Find 10 differences between these two pictures.

answers on page 58

Can you spot all 20 differences between these pictures?

answers on page 59

Awww! Minnie thinks Mickey is the sweetest thing at the Bake Sale.

Can you spot all 10 differences between these pictures?

answers on page 59

57

WHAT'S DIFFERENT?

answers for
pages 50 - 51

answers for
pages 52 - 53

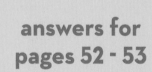

58

answers for
pages 54 - 55

answers for
pages 56 - 57

LOOK AND FIND

Minnie's picnic basket is always full of yummy surprises. See if you can find these delicious foods:

"It's a good thing we packed extra treats.
Our picnic has some unexpected guests!
Can you find them all?"

1 chipmunk   **3** bluebirds
2 puppies   **4** butterflies

LOOK AND FIND

Put on your silliest hat and join the Hat Parade! Search the scene for these parade items:

"There are more than just pretty hats in this parade!
Can you spot these dress-up delights, too?"

a yellow dress   a green collar

a purple bow   a blue bow tie

LOOK AND FIND

It's time to check the Bow-tique's inventory. Help Minnie and Daisy keep track of these supplies:

Minnie is making Figaro a new collar...with a bow, of course! Can you help her find what she needs to create it?

a spool of orange ribbon
a pair of scissors

2 yellow feathers
4 pink flowers

LOOK AND FIND

How does the gang's garden grow? With help from the April Shower Maker, naturally! Can you find everyone who has come to play in the rain?

"April showers bring yummy vegetables!
See if you can find all of these."

carrots   lettuce   cucumbers

broccoli   corn   celery

LOOK AND FIND

Mickey's taking a road trip. Can you spot these road signs and help keep him on the right track?

Welcome to ANTARCTICA

Welcome to SANDY BEACH

Welcome to the Cool FOREST

WELCOME TO THE DRY DESERT

Welcome to the RAINFOREST

Welcome to the MOUNTAINS

Welcome to the FARM

"Can you count these animals I saw along the way? Thanks, pal!"

3 bunnies
4 parrots
5 crabs
6 penguins

69

WHAT'S DIFFERENT?

The pond in the park is full of frogs. And fish, ducks, and a turtle, too!

What are the 10 differences between these two pictures?

answers on page 78

Three, two, one, blast off!

Explore these starry scenes for 10 differences.

answers on page 78

**Oh Toodles!
Where are you?**

Here comes the Super Crew to save the day!

Can you find 10 differences between these two pictures?

answers on page 79

WHAT'S DIFFERENT?

answers for pages 70 - 71

answers for pages 72 - 73

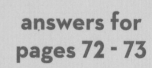

answers for
pages 74 - 75

answers for
pages 76 - 77

"Welcome!"

"When you start looking..."

"...who knows what you'll find?"

"Oh, what an adventure!"

LOOK AND FIND

Sofia loves living in the palace with her new family, though she still has a lot to learn about being a princess. Can you spot these royal objects?

"Queen **rhymes with** green. Can you find these royal rhyme pairs, too?"

gown / crown   chair / hair   suit / boot

crow / bow   fairies / berries   tea / key

83

LOOK AND FIND

Luckily, Sofia's magical amulet lets her talk to animals, so she knows which fruits are their favorites. Do you see all of these sweet treats?

"We like vegetables, too! Can you find these healthy goodies?"

green pepper   red cabbage   broccoli

carrots   lettuce   corn

LOOK AND FIND

At Royal Prep, Sofia is learning that part of being a princess is doing your best at everything you try. Will you try your best to find these school supplies?

"I'm very good at finding shapes around the classroom. Can you find them, too?"

● circle ▮ rectangle ♥ heart

▲ triangle ● oval ★ star

LOOK AND FIND

A real princess is always a good game winner...and a good loser, too! Can you spot this game-time gear?

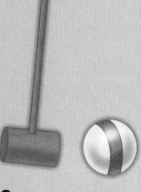

"It's fun to run and play at recess! Do you see these activities on the playground?"

bouncing   catching   throwing

reaching   jumping   kicking

89

WHAT'S DIFFERENT?

Amber loves to paint pictures, especially of herself.

WHAT'S DIFFERENT?

Sofia used to dream about living in a castle. Now she really does!

There really are 10 differences between these two pictures. Can you find them all?

answers on page 98

WHAT'S DIFFERENT?

You're invited to the royal costume ball!

Can you find 10 differences between these two party pictures?

95

Unicorns like
to dress up, too!

Find 10 differences between these two pictures.

WHAT'S DIFFERENT?

answers for
pages 90 - 91

answers for
pages 92 - 93

answers for
pages 94 - 95

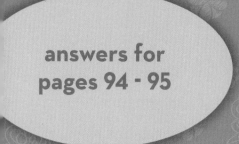

answers for
pages 96 - 97

LOOK AND FIND

What could be lovelier than a tea party in the castle garden? Why, a tea party with butterflies, of course! Try to find these colorful creatures:

"Let's flutter around the party and count these teatime things."

1 teapot   **3** Good Fairies

2 spoons   **4** princesses

101

LOOK AND FIND

Sofia is studying the ABCs of being a princess. Can you help her by finding these royal friends and family members?

A

D
dress
discu

H
horseshoe
heart

I
invitation

J
Jame
jump rop

O
orange

P
pillow
popcorn

Q

U
unicorn

V
violin

W
wand

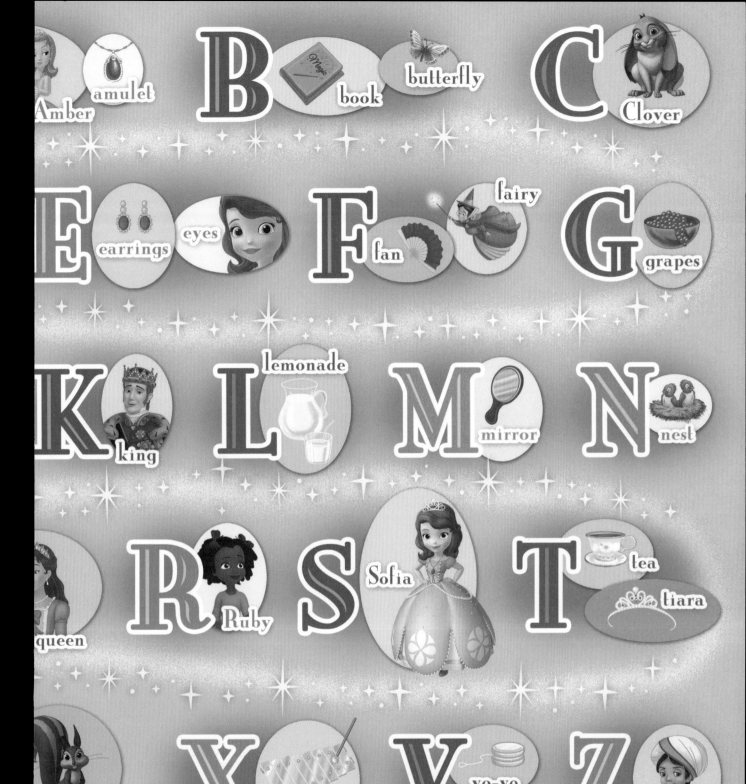

Amber — amulet

B — book — butterfly

C — Clover

E — earrings — eyes

F — fan — fairy

G — grapes

K — king

L — lemonade

M — mirror

N — nest

queen

R — Ruby

S — Sofia

T — tea — tiara

Whatnaught

X — xylophone

Y — yo-yo

Z — Zandar

"Whenever you find someone, say
the first letter of their name out loud!"

103

LOOK AND FIND

Sofia's on her way home from school...thanks to a touch of magic. Look around for more magical things at Royal Prep:

"My magical amulet is a pretty purple color. See if you can find these other colorful things outside my school."

orange bow   blue hat

green fan   red apple

LOOK AND FIND

It's the perfect princess sleepover, with Sofia's old friends and new friends together! Do you see these party must-haves?

"Party **starts with the letter** P. **Can you spot these things that start with** P, **too?**"

princess   pinecone   pajamas

popcorn   pitcher   pet

107

LOOK AND FIND

Practice makes perfect, and Sofia's waltzing is perfectly princess-y! Look for these objects around the royal ballroom:

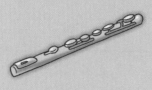

"We're having fun spotting pretty patterns.
Can you spot them, too?"

polka dots   zigzags   checkerboard

stripes   flowers   plaid

While he takes his turn, find 10 differences between these playful pictures.

answers on page 118

WHAT'S DIFFERENT?

Abra-ca-dabra and alla-kazam!
Sofia is learning magic!

But you won't need a magical spell to find 10 differences between the pictures.

answers on page 118

WHAT'S DIFFERENT?

Ruby and Jade are getting a princess makeover.

WHAT'S DIFFERENT?

Sofia needs one more Buttercup badge to earn a sunflower pin.

Be prepared to find 10 differences between these pictures.

WHAT'S DIFFERENT?

answers for
pages 110-111

answers for
pages 112 - 113

118

answers for
pages 114 - 115

answers for
pages 116 - 117

"The Doc is in!"

"Need a cuddle?"

"My hippo hunch says you'll solve every puzzle."

"I totally knew that. No, really, I did!"

"Stay cool!"

LOOK AND FIND

Ouch! Zero the alien has crash-landed. Is he OK? Look for these doctor tools Doc can use to give him a checkup:

122

"Pink is my favorite color, but I like these colors, too. Can you help me find them in Doc's clinic?"

red   green   orange

purple   yellow   blue

123

LOOK AND FIND

Sir Kirby the Knight's case of Filthy-icky-sticky disease has no chance against Doc's scrubby bubbles! Can you spot these bathtub toys?

Help Doc perform a Filthy-icky-sticky-ectomy by finding these cleaning supplies:

towel   lotion   toothpaste

bar of soap   toothbrush

LOOK AND FIND

Doc rocks! Doc, Donny, and Alma are one great band. See if you can find their musical instruments:

"It's time for an encore! Help us find a few more instruments. What sounds do they make?"

guitar   flute   harmonica

trumpet   maraca   violin

127

LOOK AND FIND

Who's that Halloween cowgirl? It's Doc! Look around to find the ghost Sebastian and this fun, spooky stuff:

"Ahoy, mateys! Can you find these feelings on the faces of Doc's jack-o-lanterns?"

happy	angry	surprised
sad	scared	sleepy

129

LOOK AND FIND

Chilly says, "Stay cool!" That's easy to do when it's snowing. Can you help Doc and her friends find the parts they need to make a perfect snowman?

"I know snow! But I could use some help finding 6 identical pairs of snowflakes. Find one, then the other matching flake."

131

Find 10 differences between these two pictures.

answers on page 140

Ricardo the race car wins again!

Zoom around to find 10 differences between these two pictures.

answers on page 140

WHAT'S DIFFERENT?

Doc fixed Bubble Monkey's bubble trouble. Let's celebrate!

Look for 10 differences between these bubbly scenes.

answers on page 141

Shhh! Quiet down, Loud Louie.
Doc's trying to sleep!

Before you say good night, search for 10 differences between the two pictures.

answers on page 141

WHAT'S DIFFERENT?

answers for
pages 132 - 133

answers for
pages 134 - 135

answers for
pages 136 - 137

answers for
pages 138 - 139

LOOK AND FIND

Doc's clinic is super-busy today! Her toys are all waiting for their checkups. Can you help Doc find these tools so she can do a good job?

"I'm as busy as a bee in a beautiful begonia, but let's take some time to see what's in these waiting room places."

on my desk   in Doc's pocket

above the sofa   next to Lambie   **143**

LOOK AND FIND

Doc and her friend Emmie love to play in the park. Can you spot the things they need for a fun day outdoors?

144

"Rudy the dog found a frog and a log.
That rhymes! Can you find these other
rhyming pairs?"

rock / sock   bee / tree

duck / truck   hat / bat   145

LOOK AND FIND

Take a look at Lambie's drawing...
then look for the letters of
Lambie's name, hidden in the
picture. Do you see them?

"My name is hidden, too. Can you find the letters that spell Stuffy?"

STUFFY

LOOK AND FIND

Five of Doc's toys need a checkup today. Can you help Hallie find and check in all of these patients?

"Those toys need a cuddle! And maybe a bandage, too. See if you can spot all of these special bandages."

149

When Doc's stethoscope starts to glow, there's magic in the air!

WHAT'S DIFFERENT?

Doc loves to play with her little brother Donny!

WHAT'S DIFFERENT?

Lambie is on the way with a special delivery: cuddles!

There are 10 differences between the pictures. Can you spot them all?

answers on page 159

Vroom-vroom!
The race is about to begin!

Zoom around and find 10 differences between these two pictures.

answers on page 159

WHAT'S DIFFERENT?

answers for
pages 150 - 151

answers for
pages 152 - 153

answers for
pages 154 - 155

answers for
pages 156 - 157

"Yo-ho, let's go!"

161

LOOK AND FIND

Ahoy, mateys! Can you help Jake and his crew find all their pirate gear?

"Looks like we're still missing a few pirate things. Do you see them anywhere?"

LOOK AND FIND

Pirate Island is full of hidden treasures. Will you dig around and see if you can find them?

"Go-go-go, me hearties, and see if you can find these things made of wood."

LOOK AND FIND

Captain Hook has a hook for every occasion...but can he find them on this messy deck? Can you?

"Oh dear, oh dear, the Captain wants these pirate things, too. Will you help me find them?"

LOOK AND FIND

Shhh! Loud music will knock down the coconut towers! See if you can find these musical instruments before Sharky and Bones do:

168

"That puny pirate Izzy is using pixie dust to fly! Can you spot these things that don't need pixie dust to move through the air?"

169

LOOK AND FIND

Jake and the crew need to hide their treasure before Captain Hook comes aboard! Quick, can you help them find it all?

"Time to rhyme! See if you can find things that rhyme with these words."

wish / fish   clock / sock   shore / door

cat / hat   best / chest   shell / bell

171

WHAT'S DIFFERENT?

Yo-ho-ho! The crew is on the move. There must be treasure nearby.

Find 10 differences between these two scenes.

answers on page 180

Jake has unlocked Skull Rock and found its treasure!

There are 10 differences between these pictures. Can you spot them?

WHAT'S DIFFERENT?

It's a coco-nutty dance party!

Can you spot 10 differences between the pictures?

answers on page 181

Jake is playing a treasure-hunting tune.

Find 10 differences between these two pictures.

answers on page 181

WHAT'S DIFFERENT?

answers for
pages 172 - 173

answers for
pages 174 - 175

180

answers for
pages 176 - 177

answers for
pages 178 - 179

LOOK AND FIND

It's a fine day for a treasure hunt. Let's get digging and find these pirate prizes:

CROCODILE COVE

SKULL ROCK

NEVER PEAK MOUNTAIN

TREASURE COVE

NEVER-SEA

The Tick Tock Croc can always find Captain Hook. Can you find these other pirates?

LOOK AND FIND

Captain Hook has a *lot* of treasure.
Can you spot some of his
fantastic favorites?

COOKING WITH
HOOK

THE
NEVER
BIRD

"The Captain sure is a puzzle to me! Let's try to figure him out by finding these puzzle pieces."

LOOK AND FIND

The Tick Tock Croc looks handsome in Hook's hat! Luckily the Captain has a few replacements. See if you can find them all.

"Pairs are things that come in twos. Can you look on the beach and help me find a pair of seashells in each of these colors?"

orange   purple   yellow

blue   pink   green

LOOK AND FIND

On Cubby's map, X marks the spot for treasure. The crew will have to find their prizes quickly, before Captain Hook spots them! Will you help?

"My bird's-eye view makes it easy to count everything around the waterfall. Can you find and count these things with me?"

1 red crab   3 green fish

2 blue birds   4 pink seashells

LOOK AND FIND

Before *Bucky* sets sail for Pirate Island, let's make sure the crew has everything a pirate needs. Look for these important items:

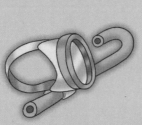

"P is for puny, pint-size pirate! Can you find these other things that start with the letter P?"

pineapple   pail   pearl

parrot   paddle   palm tree